BRENDA TIDWELL

50+ Things to do on California's Central Coast

The best beaches, hiking trails, scenic drives, wine country, marine life, and more!

First edition

This book was professionally typeset on Reedsy.
Find out more at reedsy.com

This book is dedicated to my mother, who shared her love of California's central coast with me at an early age. She and my father instilled in me a sense of wonder about the world in which we live and a desire to explore this marvelous creation.

At the beach - time you enjoyed wasting, is not wasted.

T.S. ELIOT

Contents

One

Introduction

Welcome to 50+ Things to do on California's Central Coast. Through the pages of this book, I hope to share with you some of my favorite travel destinations. The central coast of California holds special memories for me, both old and new. I grew up in California, although not on the coast, and I've been coming to this area since I was a young child, when my family would make the two hour trek to escape the summer heat of the central San Joaquin valley. The area has changed in many ways since then, but the allure of the small coastal towns I remember so well hasn't waned a bit.

This guide is by no means an exhaustive accounting of all this area has to offer. It is instead a compilation of activities and adventures for those who may be traveling to the area for the first time, or for those who need inspiration for their next adventure on the central coast. It's organized by coastal community and includes experiences from the towns and villages along the coastline stretching from Piedras Blancas, southward to the Guadalupe-Nipomo Dunes, and the inland city of Paso Robles.

This guide contains a wide range of activities, some for the young traveler, for those who are only young at heart, and for all others in between. I encourage you to experience the diverse offerings of this unique and beautiful region. I believe you will fall in love with California's central coast, as I have.

Surfer at the Pismo Beach Pier - (Photo by Tim Mossholder on Unsplash)

Two

San Simeon

William Randolph Hearst State Beach

A major reason for visiting the central coast is to enjoy its many beaches and the natural beauty which can be found there. The William Randolph Hearst State Beach at San Simeon offers a perfect opportunity to do just that. It's located off Highway 1 across from the entrance to Hearst Castle, which can be seen on the hills to the east. Once the private beach of Mr. Hearst, it was donated to San Luis Obispo county in the 1950s and was designated a state beach in 1970.

This beach is a great choice for swimming and playing in the ocean. The area is protected by San Simeon Point so you may find the surf is a bit calmer here. The waters of the central coast are much chillier than those of southern California, but you will still see children, and a few brave adults, playing in the surf without hesitation.

Pico Creek Beach

Pico Creek Beach is a great beach for beachcombing and tidepooling, It's located at Pico Avenue on the north end of San Simeon. It's a popular beach among surfers. The breaks created by the reef at the mouth of the creek make for some interesting and challenging surfing. Boards can be rented or purchased from the many surf shops on the central coast. You may also want to inquire about wetsuit rentals which can help to insulate against the colder central coast waters, especially if you'll be in the water for an extended period of time.

Whale Trail Site at San Simeon

You can follow the whale trail which has designated public viewing sites across the central coast. Whales and other marine mammals can be spotted from these and other sites during their annual migration. Gray whales migrate south from November to January, and return to the north from March to April. Humpback whales can be seen in the spring and summer months. Blue whales feed in the waters of the central coast during the summer months. More information can be found at thewhaletrail.org.

There is a designated Whale Trail viewing site located at 9415 Hearst Drive, the site of the Cavalier Resort. The Whale Trail sign is at the boardwalk where you will find three telescopes available for viewing. Interestingly, this site was used in the 1860s for shoreline whaling.

Whale Breaching - (Photo by shadowfaxone on Pixabay)

Coastal Discovery Center of San Simeon Bay

The interactive exhibits and educational displays at the Coastal Discovery Center are appropriate for both children and adults. They convey the history and culture of San Simeon and highlight the important connection between the ocean and the land. The center is a joint venture between California State Parks and the Monterey Bay National Marine Sanctuary (MBNMS), with conservancy and preservation at its heart. It is located at the William Randolph Hearst Memorial Beach at Highway 1 and SLO San Simeon Road.

The Pier at San Simeon

The San Simeon pier is one of the many public piers you will find in this region. Built in 1957, the pier extends westward into the ocean at 850 feet in length. It's a great spot for sightseeing and whale watching during their migratory periods. You can check out binoculars and Wildlife Guides from the Discovery Center before taking your stroll on the pier. Fishing is allowed, so you could witness a fisherman's catch or you may wish to throw a line in the water yourself. Fishing licenses are not required for pier fishing, but catch limits are still enforced.

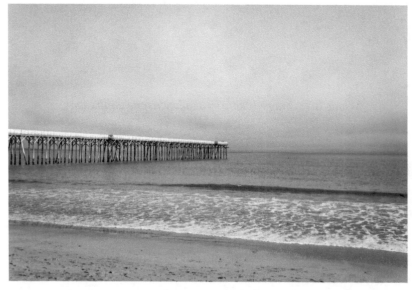

San Simeon Pier - (Photo by Gabriel Soto on Unsplash)

Piedras Blancas Light Station

Just 6 miles north of San Simeon on Highway 1 sits the historic Piedras

Blancas Light Station. It is part of the California Coastal National Monument and is managed by the Bureau of Land Management as a wildlife sanctuary and historic park. The lighthouse stands on a rocky point and was named for the white rocks below. It was illuminated for the first time in 1875. The light station is home to many species of sea lions, elephant seals, and seabirds. There are over 70 species of native plants within its 19 acres. Tours are available and should be booked online ahead of time.

Elephant Seal Rookery

Continue traveling northward on Highway 1, about 5 miles from the Piedras Blancas Light Station, to the elephant seal rookery. During winter months you can see giant elephant seals with their pups. Each year over a hundred elephant seals migrate back to the rookery for pupping. You can watch them from a safe distance, as they lie on the shore tending to their young pups. There is a designated parking area on the west side of Highway 1 with an adjacent boardwalk and viewing areas, perfect for observing the elephant seals. The best time to see them is from late November throughout the month of February.

Elephant Seals at the Rookery - (Photo by Jason Moyer on Unsplash)

Scenic Drive to Big Sur

If you're in the mood for a scenic drive and you have time to leisurely take in the sites, consider making the drive up Highway 1 from San Simeon, north to Big Sur. The 68 mile drive takes about an hour and 40 minutes one way, depending on traffic conditions, but the drive offers spectacular views of the rocky coastline. You will want to allow time to explore Big Sur and the "laid back vibe" it's famous for. Make sure to check road and weather conditions before you leave and postpone the drive if inclement weather is expected. The road is one lane both ways and is prone to rock and mudslides during wet weather.

Hearst Castle

Hearst Castle is the former retreat of publishing giant, William Randolph Hearst. The property was originally purchased by his father who had struck it rich during the California gold rush. It was used as a family camp site prior to 1919, at which time building on the site was started by the younger Hearst. He engaged the services of architect Julia Morgan of San Francisco, the first woman to own an architectural firm in California. This palatial mansion incorporates 90,000 square feet of living space in 165 rooms. It sits on 127 acres of gardens, pools, and terraces.

It was once a mecca for Hollywood royalty and other wealthy and influential people during the 1920s and 1930s. Guests included Winston Churchill, Calvin Coolidge, Howard Hughes, Charlie Chaplin, Errol Flynn, Greta Garbo, Clark Gable, and Carole Lombard, just to name a few. It is now a California State Park, open to the public for paid tours. Be sure to book ahead because it's a very popular central coast attraction.

Zebras of San Simeon

Prior to losing his fortune, William Randolph Hearst was the owner of the world's largest private zoo. As with his other exotic animals, he had zebras, native to Africa, brought to his estate. Although most of his animals were sold or donated to zoos, the zebras remained. Their offspring still roam the grounds today and can sometimes be spotted in the fenced area below the castle, on the east side of Highway 1.

Neptune Pool with Hearst Castle in the background - (Photo by Mike Hsieh on Unsplash)

Three

Cambria

Moonstone Beach

Moonstone Beach in Cambria is perhaps one of the loveliest beaches on the central coast. It was named for the small, sea-polished moonstone rocks which wash up on shore. At low tide, beachcombers can be seen scouring the beach in hopes of finding sea glass or a beautiful moonstone. Several tide pools, visible at low tide, display tiny sea creatures like crabs, sea anemones, and urchins.

Sea-Polished Pebbles on Moonstone Beach - (Photo by James Lee on Unsplash)

Moonstone Beach Boardwalk

The Moonstone Beach Boardwalk is a well maintained walkway which runs parallel to Moonstone Beach Drive. It's accessible for wheelchairs and strollers and is a popular route for joggers. The path is 1 mile from start to finish, with benches along the way for those who may want to sit, relax, and take in the scenery. To get to the beach and boardwalk, take Highway 1 to Cambria, turn onto Windsor Boulevard, then right on Moonstone Beach Drive. Parking is available near the boardwalk.

Cambria - (Photo by Michael Darnall on Pexels)

Leffingwell Landing

Leffingwell Landing lies at the northernmost end of Moonstone Beach. This day use area is a state-run park offering a boat ramp, picnic tables, barbecue pits, and restrooms. This is a great place to launch a kayak. If you're looking for a hike, there are short hiking trails leading to breathtaking scenic overlooks, and tidepools can be found along the rocky shore. To get there from the downtown area, drive north on Moonstone Beach Drive to the parking lots on the left-hand side of the street just before the Highway 1 intersection.

Shamel Park

Shamel Park is a designated Whale Trail viewing site. According to thewhaletrail.org, the entire expanse of shoreline from Shamel Park to the bluffs at Leffingwell landing create a perfect opportunity for sightings of whales and other marine life during their migratory cycles. The park is located right on the ocean at the southernmost end of Moonstone Beach. It is the site of the gentle outlet of the Santa Rosa Creek. It has amazing amenities including a green space, a large children's play area, two group day-use areas, horseshoe pits, large Santa Maria-style grills, and even a heated swimming pool for seasonal use. It has a beautiful gazebo, making this a popular spot for weddings and other celebrations.

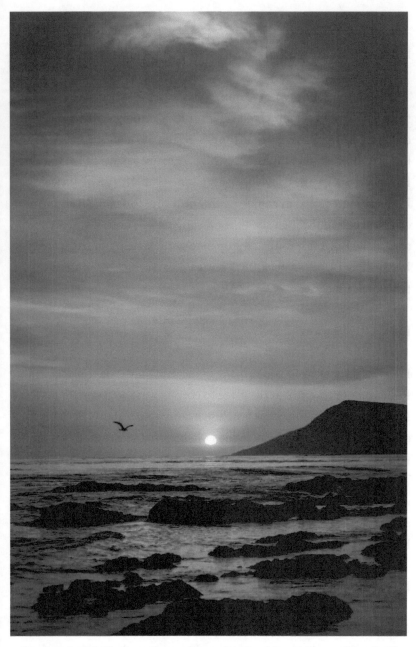

Cambria's Tide Pools at Sunset (Photo by Tim Mossholder on Unsplash)

Historic downtown Cambria

The quaint beach town of Cambria has a rich history dating back to the 1800s when it quickly sprang up as a mining town. Victorian architecture, popular at that time, strongly influenced many of the historic homes and buildings which remain today. The Cambria Historical Society has developed a walking tour with 28 historical sites. If you are interested in exploring this beautiful town, the walking tour can be accessed through the *Visit Cambria* mobile app. If you are in the area in the Fall, make sure and stop in to witness their annual Scarecrow Festival, featuring over 400 whimsical Scarecrows, each involved in their own shenanigans.

Linn's Restaurant

Definitely a favorite, if you're in the mood for home style cooking, Linn's Restaurant of Cambria is the place to go. They are well known for their hearty meals, serving breakfast, lunch, and dinner daily. Perhaps they are best known for their delicious olallieberry pies, made from vine-ripened berries grown on their own and neighboring farms in Cambria. Their fresh pies are also sold through some of the local grocery stores along the central coast. They market a line of preserves and spreads available for purchase online. Their restaurant is located in a beautiful historic building at 2277 Main Street, Cambria, CA.

Fiscalini Ranch Preserve

Once owned by the Fiscalini family, the ranch served as an active dairy farm, and later a cattle ranch, for nearly a century. Now this preserve is home to many endangered species inhabiting the seasonal marshes and wetlands. There is more than a mile of ocean bluff overlooking part of the vast Monterey Bay National Marine Sanctuary which encompasses California's Big Sur and the central coast. During migratory seasons you may be able to spot whales and elephant seals from the bluffs.

There are 437 acres of protected forest and grasslands on the ranch. Springtime is especially lovely when the wildflowers are in bloom. There are 8 trails available for exploration of this unique preserve. Along the trails are artful benches on which to rest and take in the sweeping ocean views. The office of the Friends of the Fiscalini Ranch Preserve is located at 604 Main Street, and the trail access can be found at 2799 Bluff Trail, Cambria, CA 93428.

Harmony, CA

The tiny, bohemian village of Harmony sits on just 2.5 acres. It's located 6 miles south of Cambria on Highway 1. Once the site of this region's dairy co-operative, Harmony definitely gives a nod to its roots. Here you will find whimsical cow sculptures, such as the frisbee playing cow in the courtyard. There's also a cow in a monk's robe wearing a wheel of cheese on its belt, holding an ice cream with one hoof and a butter churn with another.

Harmony is a popular stop-off for those traveling Highway 1, although it is truly a destination in itself. You can grab an ice cream at the Harmony Valley Creamery and visit the artisan galleries of the pottery and glass shops. Harmony has a beautiful chapel and gardens. The town can be rented out for weddings and other events.

Harmony Cellars

While in Harmony, you may want to stop at Harmony Cellars. This small, family-owned winery is not affiliated with the township, but is the first thing you see when you pull off the highway onto Harmony Valley Road. They offer wine tasting in their tasting room and on their patio which has beautiful views of the countryside.

Four

Cayucos

❧

Cayucos by the Sea

Cayucos is 15 miles south of Cambria on Highway 1. It has been called, "the last of the California beach towns." It truly has a small town vibe. It's the perfect place for those looking for a quiet, peaceful getaway with some beachtime thrown in. When visiting Cayucos, make sure to stop at the Brown Butter Cookie Company for some of the best ever cookies. They never disappoint.

Cayucos Murals

Scattered throughout the town are nine outdoor murals created by local artists. The Cayucos Mural Society has a downloadable map of their self-guided mural tour. It can be accessed on their site at cayucos.org, which also offers a virtual tour. A favorite is the one entitled, "Butter and Steamer Day at Cass's Cayucos Landing," painted on the side of the Cayucos Surf Shop on Ocean Avenue. It depicts the

Cayucos pioneer, James Cass, who was responsible for building the pier. This shipping port attracted steamer ships from San Francisco and Los Angeles, bringing passengers and goods to the area, and transporting the local dairy and farm products to market.

Cayucos State Beach

The beach at Cayucos is easily accessible and has nearby parking. It's a good idea to get there early, especially in the summer months, or it can be challenging to find a parking spot. The beach is dog friendly and is very walkable. Families with kids enjoy this beach which has a fun playground right on site. It's a popular beach with surfers. There are 2 surf shops near the beach where you can rent boards and wetsuits. If you're not into surfing yourself, watching the surfers can be an entertaining way to spend the day. The waves at Cayucos Beach can be majestic. On clear days you can see all the way to Morro Rock. The views up and down the coastline and the sunsets here are gorgeous.

Cayucos State Beach - (Contributed by Author)

The Cayucos Pier

The pier at Cayucos is 982 feet long and was originally constructed in 1872 for use as a shipping port. It was rebuilt in 2015 due to structural concerns. The pier is open to the public and is a popular place to fish. Beware of the playful harbor seals who have been known to steal a fisherman's catch faster than he can reel it in. It's a great place to stroll, listen to the waves passing beneath the pier, and gain a different perspective of the beautiful coastline, including views of Morro Rock to the South. If it's the right time of year, be on the lookout for whales and other migratory sea life.

Cayucos Pier - (Photo by Sixteen Miles Out on Unsplash)

Estero Bluffs State Park

North of Cayucos on Highway 1 is the Estero Bluffs State Park. This stretch of unspoiled coastal land lies between Cambria and Cayucos, comprises 353 acres, and was deeded to the State of California in 2002. The Estero Bluffs Trail, which was established in the same year, runs parallel to the rugged coastline. There are trails running east-west that connect the main trail to Highway 1, each beginning at parking turnouts on the highway. The full, one way trail length is 4 miles, but the trails from Highway 1 allow for shorter hikes. The trail is wide and flat so it's suitable for all skill levels. There is parking and easy trail access at Highway 1 and San Geronimo Road.

This trail offers spectacular views of Morro Rock and the bay. Local and migrating sea life may be spotted offshore and there are tide pools to explore. There is a beach near San Geronimo Creek but the trail to the beach is a bit rugged and rocky. Be on the lookout for the well preserved shipwreck which can be found along this hike. The trails cross native scrubs and coastal grasslands. In addition to the marine life you may see in the ocean and the varied species of sea birds residing here, you may also encounter rattlesnakes, California king snakes, salamanders, and tree frogs.

Estero Bluffs Trail - (Photo by Sixteen Miles Out on Unsplash)

Estero Bluffs Trail - (Photo by Jocelyn Allen on Unsplash)

Five

Morro Bay

⚜

Morro Rock

Undoubtedly the most defining feature of Morro Bay, majestic Morro Rock is 576 feet tall and sits at the entrance to the harbor overlooking the Pacific Ocean. It is connected to the land by a causeway which allows visitors to drive or walk to the base of the rock for a closer look. Morro Rock is one of the Nine Sisters which form a chain of volcanic peaks stretching from San Luis Obispo to Morro Bay. It is a protected California State Historical Landmark and is home to nesting Peregrine Falcons. Climbing on the rock is strictly prohibited.

You can get to Morro Rock by walking or driving north on Embarcadero, then continuing around on Coleman Drive which dead ends at the rock. Although most of the rock is surrounded by the Pacific Ocean, you can walk along the south side of the rock. At the end of the trail are thousands of stacked rocks, or cairns, that have been constructed by previous visitors to Morro Rock. If you are so inclined, you may want

25

to leave your cairn behind.

Surfers and majestic Morro Rock - (Photo by PDPhotos on Pixabay)

Beaches of Morro Bay

If you're looking for sandy beaches, Morro Bay is the place. Starting from the northern base of Morro Rock, you will find a continuous stretch of sand over six miles long. There are actually connecting beaches here, the first of which is Morro Rock Beach. Moving northward two miles, you will wander onto Morro Strand State Beach. Please be aware that dogs are prohibited on the state beach. However, if you're a dog lover do not despair, the next section of beach, Toro Creek Dog Beach, can be accessed from Toro Creek Road and Highway 1. Your dog can roam off leash here, enjoying the sand and surf alongside you.

North Point Beach, with its many tide pools, is at the northernmost end of Morro Bay. It can be accessed by the long staircase at the end of Toro Lane, or you can use the designated beach access points on Studio Drive, then walk to the tide pools at the water's edge to the north. If you choose not to descend the long stairway, there are benches on the bluffs, offering stunning views of the coastline, and in the springtime, the wildflowers here put on a spectacular show.

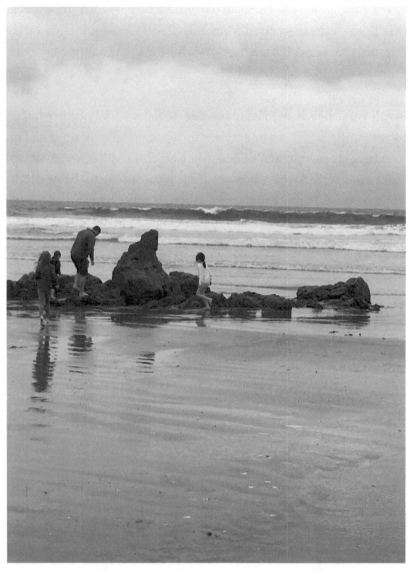

Tide Pools off Studio Drive - (Contributed by Author)

If you're in the mood for a longer stroll, the beach doesn't stop here!

You can reach Cayucos State Beach if you keep on walking to the north. This expanse of shoreline is ideal for long walks along the shore, surfing, kite flying, relaxing, building sand castles, and playing in the waves. It's a great place for beach combing, where you can find numerous shells and sand dollars at low tide. Just don't take any of the fuzzy sand dollars. They may still be alive!

Other beaches in the area include Morro Bay State Park Beach at the northeast bay and Coleman Beach along Coleman Drive, southeast of Morro Rock. Sandspit beach can only be accessed by water, but if you're craving solitude, you may want to rent a kayak or paddle board and head out to the sandspit. Don't forget to bring along any food or supplies you might need and pack out any trash. You won't find any services out there.

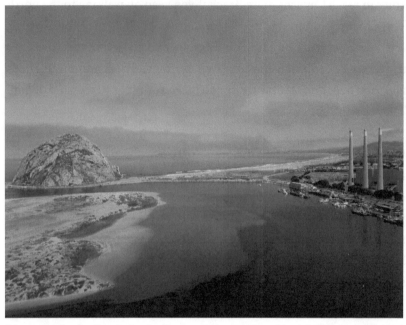

Morro Rock, the Sandspit, the Bay, and the Stacks - (Aerial Photo by Michael Olsen on Unsplash)

Mama Sea Otters and Their Pups

Regardless of the time of year, Morro Bay is a place where you can almost always find pairs of otter moms and pups. The harbor boardwalk will take you past the harbor and the best viewing areas where you can see the cute sea otters, floating on their backs and holding tightly to their pups, feeding, grooming, and teaching them to crack open crab shells with rocks and other tools. It isn't uncommon to see a raft of 20-30 sea otters with their pups, floating together in the harbor or the bay. There are also public viewing docks along the embarcadero. If you want to get closer, just not too close, you may want to check out kayak or paddleboard rentals, or take a bay tour with one of Morro Bay's boat captains.

Mama and Baby Sea Otters - (Photo by Anchor Lee on Unsplash)

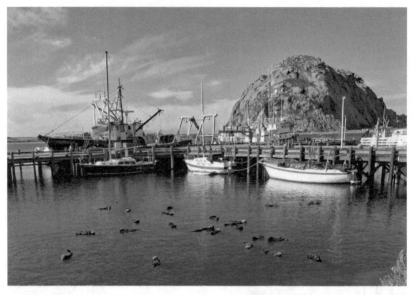

Sea Otters floating in the Harbor - (Photo by Mai Ling Thomas on Pixabay)

The Embarcadero

Morro Bay's bustling waterfront is a great place to go for shopping, dining, wine tasting, and more. Here you can buy a kite to fly on the beach, rent a bike or surrey to pedal around town, or catch a trolley to see the sights. There are surf shops where you can purchase or rent surf boards, boogie boards, kayaks, and paddleboards. You can take a picture in front of the giant clam at Giovanni's, open to resemble angel's wings, eat fish and chips on their outdoor patio with views of Morro Rock and the harbor, or buy fresh fish from their market. You can visit La Parisienne French Bakery for authentic french pastries and breads, or you can walk further down the Embarcadero and find giant cinnamon rolls made fresh that very day. Whichever direction you choose to walk, there are so many things to see. Make sure to venture down to the docks for some handmade saltwater taffy from Crills, located at 1247 Embarcadero. You won't be disappointed.

The Famous Shell Shop

This unique shop at 590 Embarcadero deserves special mention. It has been family owned and operated since 1955. They have been a mainstay on the Embarcadero, offering decorative shells and coral from around the world. They have handcrafted items made from shells, such as wind chimes, trinket boxes, jewelry, and knick knacks. The Shell Shop is beloved by many who have found treasured souvenirs here. Their slogan, "Excells in Shells," is very fitting.

Fishing

The community of Morro Bay has always been strongly linked with commercial fishing. Its fishery still exists today, as can be surmised by the many fishing boats that can be seen in the harbor. Varieties of fish commonly caught in and around Morro Bay include Lingcod, Rockfish, Tuna, Salmon, and Halibut. There are many opportunities for fishing. These include fishing charters,dock fishing, or you can try your hand at shore fishing. You can bring your own gear or you can rent from one of the bait and tackle shops in the area.

Camping

Whether tent camping or glamping, there are many opportunities to camp in the Morro Bay area. There are private parks and state campgrounds. A definite favorite, Morro Dunes RV Park, is just steps away from the beach. Campers can fall asleep to the sound of the surf. They offer tent sites or full hook ups with fire pits and picnic tables at each site. Amenities include a small variety store, restrooms with showers, laundry facilities, a dog run, horseshoe pits, and a clubhouse that can be reserved for large gatherings. Best of all, the beach is right across the dunes. Just over the footbridge is a boardwalk and bike path to Morro Rock and the Embarcadero. Be sure to make reservations ahead, as they are usually booked well in advance. Morro Dunes is located at 1700 Embarcadero.

Museum of Natural History

The Morro Bay Museum of Natural History is located south of town, within Morro Bay State Park. It boasts more than 50,000 visitors annually. The museum's exhibits are family friendly and interactive, focusing on preservation and protection of the natural habitat of the estuary, the effects of erosion, tidal forces, human forces, and geology. It is designed to appeal to both children and adults. It can be found at 20 Morro Bay State Park Road.

Morro Bay National Estuary

The Morro Bay National Estuary stretches from the southern shore of Morro Bay, all the way to Los Osos. The sand spit serves as protection from the turbulence of the ocean waves, making this a unique habitat for many plants and animals, including some endangered species. The estuary comprises 2300 acres, including 800 acres of wetlands. There are family friendly hikes, including accessible boardwalk trails. The watershed area offers more challenging hikes for experienced hikers. You can rent a kayak to explore the back bay, where two oyster farms are in operation, and the estuary channels can be accessed during high tide.

Sunset in Morro Bay (Contributed by Author)

Six

Los Osos/Baywood Park

Artists and Galleries

Los Osos and Baywood Park are well represented by the artists who call these neighboring communities home. In the back bay of Baywood Park, there is a strong focus on artisan crafts, such as one-of-a-kind blown glass and ceramic art pieces. There is even a driftwood studio where pieces of driftwood are fashioned into works of art. In Los Osos, a Pop-up gallery provides space in rotating locations for local artists to exhibit their works. Other galleries offer permanent space for art exhibitions, such as Costa Gallery where many artists using varied mediums may be on display at any given time.

Foggy Bottom Distillery

Located at 905 Los Osos Valley Road, the Foggy Bottom Distillery provides an alternative form of alcohol in an area known for its wine. Here you can sample small-batch craft spirits in their no frills outdoor tasting room which has a decidedly speak-easy feel. The distillery offers a variety of hooch to choose from, including bourbon, whiskey, gin, spiced rum, and the specialty of the house, corn whiskey. They offer flavored and seasonal varieties as well.

Los Osos Elfin Forest

If you're looking for a family friendly, or an accessible hike, you should visit the Los Osos Elfin Forest. You will not likely see any elves among the trees, but you will see dwarfed live oak trees between 4 and 20 feet tall, giving the feeling that the forest was created with elves in mind. The one mile trail is a boardwalk, suitable for strollers and wheelchairs and the hike is dog friendly if on leash. On clear days you will see panoramic views of Morro Bay, the estuary, and the mountains nearby. You may see wildlife such as deer, rabbits, and many species of birds. There are informative signs along the way and tours conducted by docents on the second Sunday and third Saturday of every month. Multiple trailheads can be accessed from 11th Street through 17th Street, off Santa Ysabela, with the easiest handicap access at 16th Street.

Sweet Springs Nature Preserve

If you're looking to do some bird watching, Sweet Springs Nature Preserve should be your destination. This 32 acre site, located off Ramona Avenue in Los Osos, offers exceptional birding opportunities. The Morro Coast Audubon Society owns and manages this beautiful property, providing a haven for birds and bird watchers since 1989. There have been sightings of over 350 bird species from this site, including the California Quail, the American White Heron, the Canada Goose, the Brown Pelican, the Spotted Sandpiper, and the Bald Eagle. Visitors can enjoy hiking trails with lovely views of Morro Bay with majestic Morro Rock in the distance. Please note that dogs are not allowed due to the many vulnerable ground nesting birds at the preserve.

Montaña de Oro State Park

Located at 3550 Pecho Valley Road, Montaña de Oro State Park has much to offer. There are beautiful sandy beaches, spectacular views from rugged cliffs, hills, and coastal plains, numerous tidepools, and miles of hiking trails. A great place for a day trip, the park also offers a campground with options for traditional and equestrian camping, with trail riding, and mountain biking opportunities. Beautiful Spooner's Cove is right across from the campground. This gorgeous beach is the only dog friendly beach in the park, but leashes are required. Rumor has it, Spooner's Cove, once called Smuggler's Cove, was used as a port for smugglers bringing Canadian Whiskey into the area during prohibition.

Montaña de Oro State Park - (Photo by Kenzo Yokoyama on Unsplash)

Bluff Trail

This easy hiking trail in Montaña de Oro State Park is handicap accessible and kid friendly. It's 4.1 miles round trip and takes about 1.5 hours. The trail leads along the bluff next to the ocean with amazing panoramic views, beach access points, and tide pools. This is another great place to see whales and other marine mammals offshore during their migratory periods. In the Spring, the beautiful California poppies add a pop of color to the landscape. There are parking lots next to the trail along Pecho Valley Road, including a lot at Spooner's Cove. Unfortunately, dogs are not allowed on this trail hike.

Bluff Trail - (Photo by Ronan Furuta on Unsplash)

Seven

San Luis Obispo

Downtown San Luis Obispo (SLO)

With its tree-lined streets, historic buildings, cafes, restaurants, wine bars, microbreweries, and an eclectic assortment of shops, downtown San Luis Obispo has something for everyone. This vibrant college town is home to California Polytechnic State University, better known as Cal Poly. Here you will find students looking to unwind, and others still in study mode at the corner cafe. There are people from all walks of life who live and visit here, looking for the SLO life. Many of the downtown activities are centered on and around Higuera Street. Every Thursday night from 6:00 to 9:00, its five block long Farmer's Market brings together over 100 vendors displaying their farm fresh produce, artisan crafts, delicious baked items, mouthwatering foods, and live entertainment. Due to the amazing weather in SLO, the market can be held year round.

Farmer's Market - (Photo by Shelley Pauls on Unsplash)

Bubblegum Alley

If you've ever wanted to leave your mark on the world, Bubblegum Alley off of Higuera Street in SLO may just afford you that opportunity. This 70 foot long pedestrian alleyway has to be one of the oddest tourist attractions to date. It's tucked away between Garden and Broad, and is easy to miss unless you're looking for it. The walls of the alleyway are plastered with innumerable globs of multi-colored ABC (already been chewed) gum. There are varied accounts of how the tradition started. Some believe it began as a local high school graduation stunt in the 1940s, others say it was started by students from Cal Poly during the 1950s. The city decided to clean up the alley in the 1970s, but soon after, the colorful blobs of gum began to reaccumulate. What color

42

bubblegum will you choose to add to Bubblegum Alley?

San Luis Obispo Museum of Art

Free to the public, the SLO Museum of Art is truly accessible to all. It's located downtown at 1010 Broad Street, off Higuera, at the west end of Mission Plaza. Exhibitions include works with varied artistic styles from esteemed visual artists of California and across the globe. They house a permanent collection, and have temporary exhibits which change monthly. They offer art classes for varied age groups and skill levels, lectures, events, and concerts.

San Luis Obispo Children's Museum

Located at 1010 Nipomo Street, the SLO Children's Museum serves nearly 50,000 guests per year. The interactive exhibits provide hands-on learning through play. There are three stories and an outdoor play area for families and children to explore and enjoy, creating unique opportunities to interact and make lasting memories. They offer scheduled educational activities and programs each week. The SLO Children's Museum is recommended for children ages 1-10.

Edna Valley

Just 10 minutes southeast of downtown San Luis Obispo lies the pastoral community of Edna Valley. This area has established itself as an American Viticultural Area, best known for Chardonnay, Pinot Noir, and Syrah. This wine trail begins just past the SLO County Regional Airport on Highway 227.

Tolosa winery will be one of the first you'll see. Their beautiful tasting room, outdoor patio, and award winning wines make for a great start to your wine tasting journey. If a barrel tasting tour interests you, be sure to book this ahead of time. Down the road at Old Edna, you will find a different, but equally satisfying experience at Sextant. Here, at their 100+ year old former General Store, you can order lunch or enjoy a charcuterie board from their gourmet deli. You can sidle up to their handmade bar or enjoy a tasting on their dog-friendly outdoor patio. This site at Old Edna is rich with history, so leave some time to explore their 2 acre townsite.

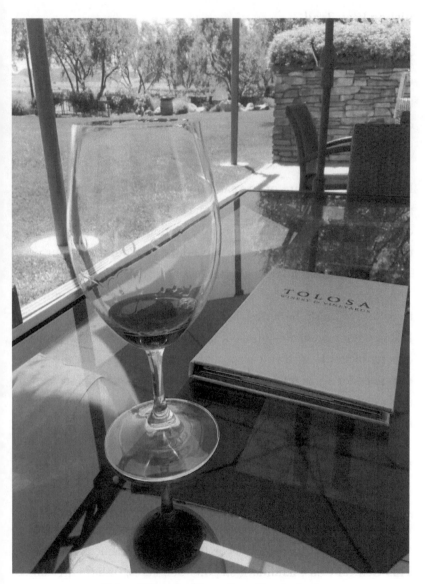

Tolosa Winery - (Contributed by Author)

Bishop Peak Trail

Bishop Peak is the most prominent of the mountains in the San Luis Obispo area. Standing at 1559 feet, it's the tallest of the Nine Sisters, the chain of volcanic Morros stretching from SLO to Morro Bay. In comparison, Bishop Peak dwarfs its little sister, Morro Rock, which stands at 576 feet.

Bishop Peak trails are open year round and include a moderate to rigorous hike to the summit, which on clear days offers amazing views of the coastline and SLO. At four miles round trip, this out and back trail should take approximately two hours, depending on your pace. The Felsman Loop offers a shorter, easy to moderate intensity hike. This loop trail is 1.7 miles and takes about an hour and 15 minutes from start to finish. Both trails begin off Patricia Drive in SLO, with the Felsman Loop branching off from the Bishop Peak Trail at just under a quarter of a mile in. If you are feeling energetic, the two trails can be combined for a 5.75 mile hike. These trails are very popular, so you will likely encounter other hikers along the way. Dogs are permitted but must be on leash.

Madonna Inn

The Madonna Inn, located at 100 Madonna Road, was originally opened in 1958 by Alex and Phyllis Madonna. With its Swiss Alps style exterior, It's best known for its kitschy decor and elaborate, themed guest rooms. This Central Coast landmark sits on 1500 acres. It has entertained many celebrities and is a favorite destination for honeymooners and romantics. There are 110, one-of-a-kind guestrooms, including: "Caveman," with its stone floors and walls, and waterfall shower and sinks; the secluded "Madonna Suite," with its custom pink rose carpet, massive stone fireplace, and waterfall shower; and "Yahoo," with its rock shower and buckboard style bed, complete with wagon wheels.

The Inn is complete with conference facilities. It has a cocktail lounge, and their steakhouse and cafe offer delicious meals. The onsite bakery serves delectables, like their multi-layer specialty cakes, with slices too large not to share. While you're there, don't forget to check out the famous stone urinal in the men's room, complete with automatic waterfall feature.

Mission San Luis Obispo

Located at 751 Palm Street, Mission San Luis Obispo was founded in 1772 by Junipero Serra. Father Serra was a Roman Catholic Priest of the Franciscan order who is credited for founding nine of the 21 Spanish missions in California. Built in the Spanish missionary adobe style, it overlooks beautiful San Luis Creek. There is a courtyard with a rose garden and grapevines, shaded by oak trees. A museum is housed in the former residence quarters, which highlights the Native American culture of this area, as well as the history of the Spanish missionaries. Mass is still held daily at this site.

Eight

Avila Beach

Downtown Avila Beach

Avila Beach is yet another beautiful, quintessential beach town on the central California coast. Tucked behind the coastal mountains, it's off the beaten path, with just one road in and out. There's so much packed into this little town that once you've found this gem, you'll keep coming back, just as others have. From Highway 101, take the Avila Beach Drive exit and follow the road for about 2.5 miles into the heart of the town. If you're planning a visit here it's best to arrive early, because parking fills up quickly, especially on the weekends and throughout the summer.

There are many beachfront shops and dining options along Front Street. Custom House restaurant has options for indoor dining or you can opt for their outdoor, dog-friendly patio. The atmosphere is casual, with top-notch service and a variety of tasty food choices, including steak, fresh seafood, and salads. They are open for breakfast, lunch, and dinner, daily.

Bob Jones Trail

This paved and well maintained trail, also referred to as the City to the Sea Trail, is a popular bike and walking path, suitable for all skill levels. You can access the trailhead near the parking lot on Ontario Road, just off Highway 101. It meanders along the San Luis Obispo Creek, past the fields of the Avila Valley Barn. The trail ends at downtown Avila Beach and if you continue to the end of the pier, the entire trail is 3 miles in length.

Central Coast Aquarium

Located at 50 San Juan Street in Avila Beach, the Central Coast Aquarium provides an up close look at some of the marine life that inhabit the waters of the central coast. This small, nonprofit aquarium focuses on ocean stewardship and offers programs for local schools, and summer day camps to promote continued interest and learning. Docent-led tours and feeding tours are available. Be sure to check their hours of operation before your visit.

Beaches

There are three beaches near Avila. At the main beach off Front Street, you'll find the perfect place to relax and enjoy the sun. Avila Beach is usually warmer than the other beaches on the central coast. It faces the South, overlooking the sheltered San Luis Bay. To the east is Fossil Point and to the west is Point San Luis, which rises to 600 feet in elevation, creating a break from the prevailing winds from the north. Dogs are not allowed on this beach between 10:00 a.m. and 5:00 p.m. For dog-friendly options, Port San Luis, to the west of Avila Beach, offers two beach options, including Olde Port Beach, and Fisherman's beach, where dogs are allowed to roam off-leash. The largest of the two beaches, Olde Port Beach has a ramp where you can launch and load your boat or kayak.

Sunset on the beach - (Photo by SugJeong from Pixabay)

Piers

There are three piers in San Luis Bay. Two are open to the public, and the other is utilized by Cal Poly for marine research, therefore, public access is prohibited. The Avila Beach pier extends 1,685 feet in length. Constructed in 1908, it was originally used as a wharf for fishing and passenger vessels. Today it's a popular site for fishing, strolling, viewing the beautiful San Luis Bay, and whale-watching during the migratory seasons. The Harford pier to the west is 1,320 feet in length, and was built by John Harford in 1878. There is a breakwater at Point San Luis that provides shelter for the pier, which is still used by commercial fishing vessels. Public fishing is allowed here, and remember, you don't need a fishing license to fish from any of the piers. You can drive your vehicle on the Harford Pier, which is prohibited on most piers in California. For a unique dining experience with the best views over the water, visit the Olde Port Inn, located directly on the Harford Pier.

Avila Beach Pier - (Photo by Kevin Dunlap on Unsplash)

Pirate's Cove

Tucked away between Avila Beach and Shell Beach, Pirate's Cove is the only clothing-optional beach along the central coast. Its name was inspired by the legendary smugglers and rum-runners who would stash their booty in the many caves along this stretch of coastline. From Avila Beach Drive, take Cave Landing Road and follow it to the end where the main parking lot can be found. From there, take the path leading east to the sign that will direct the way to the main cave and to the beach. The main cave is a tunnel leading through rock to an amazing vantage point for beautiful San Luis Bay and the Pacific Ocean.

Avila Valley and See Canyon

Home to apple orchards and wineries, there are things to see and do in Avila Valley and See Canyon year round, but Fall is arguably the best time to visit. Apple season runs September to December and brings a harvest of fresh, crisp apples of many varieties. Located on Avila Beach Drive, and along See Canyon Road, the Avila Apple Trail showcases tree ripened apples, pastries, pies, and other apple products. Apple cider is a definite favorite, with some locations offering hard cider, and apple wines, both still and sparkling. Open year round, Avila Valley Barn at 560 Avila Beach Drive offers seasonal, locally grown fruits and vegetables. They have a petting zoo, which is a favorite with kids, or you can stop for an ice cream, or to grab lunch at their SmokeHouse and Chicken Shack on your way to the beach.

Hot Springs

There are two resorts near Avila Beach which have natural mineral hot springs on site. These springs were first discovered by drillers in search of oil, in 1886 at Sycamore Mineral Springs, and at Avila Hot Springs in 1907. Long believed to have curative powers, both resorts have entertained many guests hoping to soak their cares away. Sycamore Springs was a popular stop for Hollywood royalty en route to

Hearst Castle in the 1920s and 1930s. Each resort offers spa treatments and massage therapy services, and overnight accommodations. Avila Springs is family friendly with more rustic options, including cabins for up to four guests, tent camping, and RV sites for vehicles under 25 feet. Sycamore Springs has guest rooms and suites, each with their own private mineral spring hot tub.

Point San Luis Lighthouse

The lighthouse at Port San Luis was constructed in 1890, following the sinking of the steamship, Queen of the Pacific, two years earlier. The large ship began taking on water about 15 miles from Port Harford (later renamed Port San Luis). The captain was slowly steaming in, navigating the rocky coastline, desperately searching for the harbor in the dark, pre-dawn hours when it ran aground some 500 feet from the pier. This incident highlighted the need for a beacon in this location.

This beautiful Victorian style Lighthouse has been meticulously restored and is available for tours every Wednesday and Saturday, with advance reservations required. The lighthouse is not accessible by private car, but there are adventurous options for getting there. These include a docent-led hike along the Pecho Coast Trail, or you may choose to arrive by kayak or paddleboard. A van tour is also available for those seeking a less labor intensive option for their visit to the lighthouse. However you choose to get there, you will be awed by the spectacular views of the coastline, and entranced by the beauty of this historically important place.

Port San Luis Lighthouse - (Photo by Kevin Dunlap on Unsplash)

Nine

Pismo Beach

Downtown Pismo Beach

Pismo Beach is yet another iconic California central coast town. There is an energetic vibe in this community, where people come to participate in the many events and activities that await them here. The downtown area is centered around the newly refurbished Pismo Beach Pier and Promenade. Every Wednesday evening from April to October, the Farmer's Market brings people together here. There are vendors with fresh produce, jewelry, local artists' offerings, and live music. The downtown area boasts a variety of surf shops, bike and surrey rentals, gift and specialty boutiques, and amazing cafes and restaurants.

The city is host to many annual celebrations and events. This includes their annual Clam Festival which occurs over three days every October. The city was once known as the "Clam Capital of the World," and although the clams have all but disappeared, the city continues to celebrate their historical impact on the community of Pismo Beach.

The city's annual Fourth of July celebration, complete with an amazing fireworks display, keeps people coming back year after year. The Classic at Pismo Beach car show, an annual tradition since the 1980's, features vintage automobiles from all over the United States. The event features a live auction to raise money for worthy charities. Another annual occurrence, the St. Anthony Celebration is held in Pismo Beach each year, bringing together generations of Portuguese families for this religious observance. These are but a few of the many events that occur annually in this vibrant city.

Pismo Beach and Pier - (Photo by Tobias Smietana on Unsplash)

Pismo Pier

The Pismo Pier has had a long history, fraught with ongoing wear from the swells of the sea, and even outright destruction from many years of storm activity. Prior to the establishment of Pismo Beach in 1891, the Pismo Wharf was built in 1882 at the site of the current pier. Extending 1,740 feet in length, this working wharf had two warehouses near its entrance, and a handcar track for moving cargo from end to end. A dancehall was built near the wharf in 1895 and thrived until the 1920's. The pier, however, was demolished in 1905 by a severe storm.

A second pier, which was longer and wider, was built in 1924 and full public access was allowed. Shortly after it was completed, 500 feet at the end of the pier was lost to a storm. It suffered more storm damage in 1952 when it lost 150 feet from the far end of the pier. The huge pilings which held up the end of the pier washed ashore and were retrieved from the beach. Repairs were completed and the pier was once again operational.

A complete refurbishment was conducted in 1985 after the pier was significantly damaged by the El Nino storms of 1983. More recently, concerns over the pier's structural integrity were raised and the pier underwent another complete renovation, along with the Promenade area in front of the pier. Now, at 1,370 feet in length, the pier is not only structurally sound, but it is aesthetically beautiful. The pier has several cantilevered extended deck areas, perfect for fishing, whale watching during their migratory season, and sight-seeing. There are three classic airstream trailers on the pier serving as food trucks, giving even more reason to enjoy a stroll on the pier.

Pismo Beach Pier - (Photo by John Edmonds on Pixabay)

Pismo State Beach

At around 17 miles in length, Pismo State Beach is a beautiful sandy beach, stretching across the coastal towns of Pismo Beach, Grover Beach, and Oceano. It's a great beach for long strolls or jogs, swimming, surfing, bodyboarding, sunbathing, fishing, and watching the sunset. This expansive public beach is maintained by the California Department of Parks and Recreation.

Oceano Dunes

At the southern end of Pismo Beach, Oceano Dunes State Vehicular Recreation Area is the only place in California where you can drive and camp on the beach. The entrance is located at 100 Pier Avenue in Oceano. The vast sandy dunes provide a perfect haven for off-road vehicle enthusiasts and their four wheel drives, ATVs, and dune buggies. Camping is rustic, with some port-a-potties available, so self-contained vehicles are advised. It is common, however, for campers to find themselves stuck and needing to be pulled out of the sand. You will likely find helpful people willing to pull you out, for a fee. Camping is on a limited basis, so be sure to make reservations ahead of time.

Dinosaur Caves Park

There is a great story behind the name and theme of this oceanfront, kid friendly park in the Shell Beach area of Pismo Beach. A large, concrete dinosaur was built on this site in the 1940's as a tourist attraction. There was a tunnel in the tail of the dinosaur, leading to a sea cavern below. The dinosaur and the sea cavern have since collapsed, but the existing park pays homage to its predecessor with dinosaur themed playground equipment. There are public restrooms, picnic tables, and hiking trails along the cliffs. The small beach below, with its beautiful caves and arch formations, is unfortunately no longer accessible from the cliffs at Dinosaur Caves Park. It is possible to kayak here from Eldwayen Park, or Margo Dodd Park. You can access the parking lot of Dinosaur Caves Park just off Price Street on Cliff Avenue.

Eldwayen Ocean Park

Beautiful Eldwayen Park is located on Ocean Boulevard along the cliffs of the Shell Beach area. It spans approximately one mile. At low tide, there are tidepools teeming with sea life, including crabs, sea anemones, limpets, starfish, and sea urchins. This long, narrow stretch of beach can be accessed by staircase. One can be found near the grassy park off Ocean Boulevard near Morro Avenue. The other stairway is located to the north at Vista del Mar Avenue. This is a great spot to put in a kayak if you wish to explore the caves and arches below Dinosaur Caves Park, and nearby Margo Dodd Park. You can find parking on the street on Ocean Boulevard.

Margo Dodd Park

This beautiful park is adjacent to Dinosaur Caves Park. It has a small grassy area, a beautiful gazebo, picnic tables, and benches that are perfectly placed to take in the amazing view of the sea and coastline. There are arches and caves on the beach below. Tidepools are visible at low tide, offering a glimpse of the tiny sea life that inhabit them. This is a good place to put in a kayak if you wish to explore the small beach, caves, and arches at Dinosaur Caves Park. You can find the stairs to Margo Dodd Beach Park at Pier Avenue and Ocean Boulevard, two blocks north of the gazebo. Parking is along Ocean Boulevard, or in the public lot at Dinosaur Caves Park.

Pismo State Beach Monarch Butterfly Grove

There are only five places in California where monarch butterflies return annually during their migration period. Pismo Beach happens to be one of them. Thousands of these black and orange beauties gather on the branches of the eucalyptus trees located in the grove at 400 S. Dolliver. This amazing spectacle should not be missed and can be witnessed from October to February of each year.

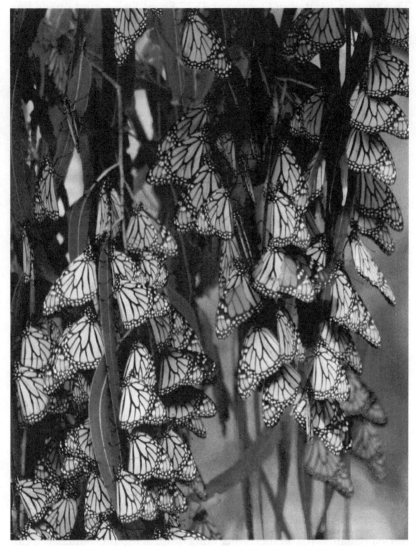

Pismo State Beach Monarch Butterfly Grove - (Photo by Jan Dommerholt on Unsplash)

The Great American Melodrama and Vaudeville

This theater, located in Oceano at 1827 Front Street, first opened its doors in 1975. Since that time, its theater group has offered high quality productions, including comedies, musicals, and classic melodramas where theater-goers are encouraged to boo and hiss at the villian. Their productions employ professionally trained actors, and a vaudeville revue is presented at the conclusion of every show, so audiences are essentially treated to a double feature. As reported on their website, performances are fun for the entire family, aged 4 to 104. With cabaret style seating available, advance tickets can be purchased at their box office and online.

Guadalupe-Nipomo Dunes

South of Oceano lies the Guadalupe-Nipomo Dunes Wildlife Refuge. The dunes complex encompasses 20,000 acres along an 18 mile stretch of sand in southwest San Luis Obispo county and northwest Santa Barbara County. The refuge was established for conservation of these coastal dunes and wetlands. The area is home to many plants and animals, some of which are considered threatened or endangered.

Here you will find pristine beaches and freshwater lagoons. There are miles of hiking trails. Interestingly, this area was used by Cecil D. DeMille in his 1923 silent technicolor film, "The 10 Commandments." An elaborate film set was created, and rather than transport the set back to Hollywood, it was dismantled and buried in the sand. Many of the buried remains are still there, including those of a giant sphinx. You can learn more about this, see an exhibit of movie artifacts, and discover where to find the dune access points at the Dunes Center, located at 1065 Guadalupe Street, Guadalupe, CA.

Ten

Paso Robles

Downtown Paso Robles

A trip to the California central coast would not be complete without at least a day trip to Paso Robles. Although it does not border the ocean, it's a short 24 mile scenic drive to its closest beach. It is situated midway between San Francisco and Los Angeles on coastal Highway 101. Its historic downtown area is fun to explore with its artisan shops and downtown wine district featuring more than 20 wineries.

Wine tasting

Paso Robles has earned its reputation as a premier destination for wine enthusiasts. With over 200 wineries in the area, wine tasting opportunities abound. Its wine country stretches along highway 46 and through the winding back roads of Paso Robles with offerings ranging from small boutique wineries, to world-class establishments. There are many commercial wine tour companies operating in the area for those who wish to leave the driving to someone else. Be aware that reservations for tastings may be required at some wineries, such as favored Daou Vineyards which offers culinary pairings with their tastings. If you haven't reserved ahead, no need to worry, there are plenty of vineyards offering drop-in wine tasting experiences.

Beautiful Vineyard - (Photo by Pixabay)

Sensorio

Located at 4680 Highway 46 East in the heart of wine country, the Light at Sensorio is an experience not to be missed. Works of artist Bruce Munro, both the Field of Light and Light Towers, comprise the walk-through exhibit. Featured are 15 acres of illuminated rolling landscape and a more recent installation consisting of 69 towers constructed of more than 17,000 wine bottles, a nod to the local wine industry, all lit with fiber optics. As you may have guessed, the exhibit is best viewed after dark, so be sure to pack a sweater or jacket, because even when it's hot here during the day, it usually cools off in the evening.

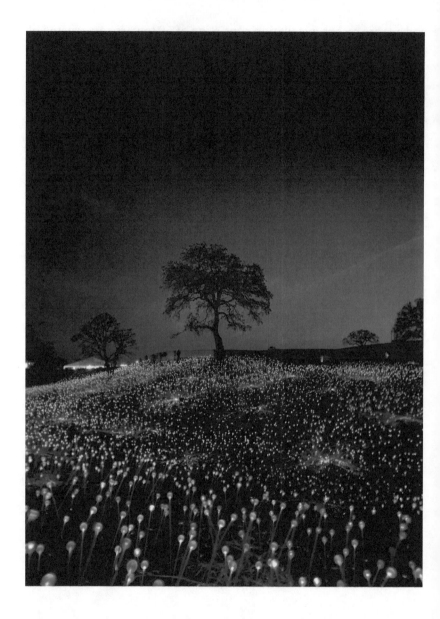

Photo by Kevin Lanceplaine on Unsplash

Vina Robles Amphitheater

Vina Robles winery has created a unique venue, providing an intimate setting for concert-goers. Since opening in 2013, the amphitheater has drawn many headliners from all genres, to its picturesque location on a beautiful Paso Robles hillside. It has established itself as a preeminent outdoor platform for entertainment, with concert season from April to November. Also known for their exceptional wines, if you are a wine club member, you may be able to enjoy a pre-show happy hour. Vina Robles is located at 3800 Mill Road.

Paso Robles Hot Springs

After a full day of sight-seeing and wine tasting, you may wish to soak away your cares in the mineral-rich waters of one of the three public hot springs located in Paso Robles. For over a century people have come to this area to experience what was believed to be the healing properties of its natural hot springs. Some of the springs in the area had to be diverted due to city planning and growth, such as the old bath house spring site, now home to the city's government buildings.

You may want to try all three public locations. In addition to their hot springs, each offers other unique and vastly different experiences. River Oaks Hot Springs Spa, located in a residential area at 800 Clubhouse Drive, offers massage therapy services and spa treatments. The remote Franklin Hot Springs at 3015 Creston Road in northeast Paso Robles has a freshwater lake, just right for largemouth bass fishing. Paso Robles Inn, also on the northeast side at 1103 Spring Street, offers overnight stays in one of 98 rooms in its historic hotel.

Mission San Miguel Arcángel

A short, nine mile drive north on Highway 101 from Paso Robles will

50+ Things to do on California's Central Coast

lead you to Mission San Miguel Arcángel. Founded in 1797, it is one of nine California missions established by Father Junipero Serra of the Franciscan order. This State and National Historic Landmark is located at 775 Mission St, San Miguel, CA. The frescoes within the church are works of the original artists, completed over 200 years ago. Much of the original buildings remain unchanged. Docent-led museum tours are available with advanced scheduling or you can opt for a self-guided tour.

Eleven

Conclusion

I thank you for taking this journey down the central coast of California with me. I hope you've had as much fun as I have. There are so many things to see and do in this beautiful place, that I could have gone on and on. I certainly hope you will find the ideas listed in this guide to be helpful and inspiring as you plan your next trip or adventure on the central coast. As you explore its many wonders, you will no doubt discover your own favorite things to do.

If you have found this book to be helpful, I would appreciate it if you would leave a favorable review on Amazon. Happy Travels to you and yours!

Twelve

Resources

All Trails, LLC. (2022). *Montaña de Oro bluff trail.* Retrieved October 13, 2022, from
   https://www.alltrails.com/trail/us/california/montana-de-oro-bluff
-trail

Avila Beach Tourism Alliance. (2022, October 7). *Avila Beach official visitor guide: Avila Beach,*
   CA. Retrieved October 13, 2022, from https://www.visitavilabeach.c
om

California Beaches. (n.d.). *The info you need on all the best beaches in California.* Retrieved
   October 13, 2022, from https://www.californiabeaches.com

Cayucos Chamber of Commerce. (2022). *Where the old west meets the ocean.* Retrieved
   October 13, 2022, from https://www.cayucoschamber.com

Cayucos Mural Society. (n.d.). *Cayucos mural society.* Retrieved October 13, 2022, from
  http://cayucos.org/muralsociety/index.html

County of San Luis Obispo Parks & Recreation. (n.d.). *Bishop Peak Natural Area.* Retrieved
  October 13, 2022, from https://slocountyparks.com/trails/bishop-peak-natural-area

Downtown SLO. (2022). *Downtown San Luis Obispo: You belong here.* Retrieved October 13,
  2022, from https://downtownslo.com

Friends of the Fiscalini Ranch Preserve. (2022). *Welcome to the Fiscalini Ranch Preserve.*
  Retrieved October 13, 2022, from https://www.fiscaliniranchpreserve.org

The Great American Melodrama and Vaudeville. (n.d.). Retrieved October 13, 2022, from
  https://www.americanmelodrama.com

Guadalupe-Nipomo Dunes Center. (2020). *Dunes center.* Retrieved October 13, 2022, from
  http://www.dunescenter.org

Harmony, CA. (n.d.). *Town of Harmony.* Retrieved October 13, 2022, from
  http://harmonytown.com

Highway 1 Road Trip. (2021, December 20). *Estero bluffs state park.*

Retrieved October 13,
   2022, from https://highway1roadtrip.com/things-to-do/estero-bluf
fs-state-park

Jones, K. (2022, February 1). Pier fishing in California: Pismo Beach
pier. Retrieved October
   13, 2022, from https://www.pierfishing.com/pismo-beach-pier

Visit Morro Bay. (n.d.). *Morro Bay: Things to do*. Retrieved October 13,
2022, from
   https://www.morrobay.org/things-to-do

Morro Coast Audubon Society. (2021). *Sweet springs nature preserve*.
Retrieved October 13,
   2022, from https://www.morrocoastaudubon.org/p/sweet-springs-
nature-
   preserve.html

National Ocean Service. (2022, June 1). *Monterey Bay National Marine
Sanctuary: Coastal
   Discovery Center at San Simeon Bay*. Retrieved October 13, 2022, from
   https://montereybay.noaa.gov/vc/cdc

San Simeon Chamber of Commerce. (2022). *What to do in San Simeon,
California*. Visit San
   Simeon. Retrieved October 13, 2022, from https://visitsansimeonca.
com/what-to-do

Sensorio Paso Robles. (2021). *Bruce Munro: Light at Sensorio*. Retrieved
October 13, 2022,
   from https://sensoriopaso.com

Travel Paso. (2020). *Out and about: Paso Robles.* Retrieved October 13, 2022, from
   https://www.travelpaso.com/things-to-do

U.S. Fish and Wildlife Service. (2022, June 27). *Guadalupe-Nipomo Dunes National Wildlife*
   Refuge. Retrieved October 14, 2022, from https://www.fws.gov/refuge/guadalupe-
   nipomo-dunes

Visit Cambria. (2022, August 1). *Welcome to Cambria.* Retrieved October 13, 2022, from
   https://visitcambriaca.com

The Whale Trail. (2021). *The Whale Trail.* Retrieved October 13, 2022, from
   https://thewhaletrail.org

Yadegaran, J. (2016, August 12). *Paso Robles: Three spots to soak in hot mineral springs.* The
   Mercury News. Retrieved October 13, 2022, from
   https://www.mercurynews.com/2014/03/07/paso-robles-three-spots-to-soak-in-
   hot-mineral-springs

Made in United States
Troutdale, OR
04/23/2024

19388830R00046